WHAT I DID IN CUBA

PAUL MYERS

WHAT I DID IN CUBA

Copyright © 2008 by Paul Myers.

All rights reserved.

ISBN 978-1-8479948-5-1

www.whatididonmyholidays.net

Contents

Introduction 1

Welcome to Cuba 4

Havana 7

Varadero 39

Cayo Coco 60

Swimming With Dolphins 65

Kim's Story 68

Trinidad 74

Escape to Havana 86

Introduction

The tale you are about to read covers three weeks of unplanned adventure across Cuba starting in the last days of 1994. A time known as the 'Special Period'. Soviet big brother was no longer there to lend a helping hand and the nation was imploding. Food was short, oil supplies were drying up, the country was at the beginning of a new revolution as a self sustaining nation, where tourism would be one of the home resources that Cuba would need to learn how to exploit effectively. There were no 'Rough Guide to Cuba' or 'Lonely Planet' guides back then to help us navigate straight to the best bits or tell us what to avoid. All we had was a very poor, shiny, purple covered, independently published guidebook. It seemed out of date at the time (aren't all guidebooks now we have the Internet?) and had terrible hand drawn maps that were more hindrance than help. We gave it away before we even left Cuba. It was that useless.

The other 50% of the 'we' I talk of is my girlfriend of the time Alison, the artist formally known as Betty Boo. We'd trekked in Nepal, stayed with tribes-people in the Thai jungle and decided on giving Cuba a spin as we still didn't know any non-Cubans who had been there. And at the time that seemed like a good enough reason as any.

Another key cast member in this chronicle is the artist still known as Gary Glitter. Though subsequent unfortunate events mean he is less well known for his artistry now than he was at the time of writing. It is important to bear in mind that the bulk of this work was first written back in the last century not long after the events depicted occurred and I have purposely not altered the writing in spite of what has happened with him since. That would be too easy with the benefit of hindsight and the historic authenticity of this journal would be lost forever. Also I really don't want to play with the heads of the legions of historians not yet born who may one day debate this book's importance on the shape of civilisation or the destruction of moral values eventually causing the last inhabitants of this, our only Earth to decamp to another world far, far away. Anyway you get my drift. Let's hope it doesn't come to that, eh?

What I Did in Cuba is part of a yet to be released work covering more of the same, but in different places with different people. The reason I am publishing this episode earlier than the rest of the book is that my literary agent for the last ten years, Monty Beigelstern has twice threatened to commit suicide if I don't release something before he dies. And so this, if you like, has become the first single from the forthcoming album. In the following pages you will come with me through Cuba from top to tail and learn, laugh and maybe cry a little too. Who knows, maybe you're having a bad day? This is a tale of three weeks in the Sunshine Socialist State where extortion, confrontation, dolphins, bad food and how I met The Leader by complete accident are part of what became a story worth sharing. And all we wanted at the time was a nice quiet, boring beach holiday.

All the events and people in this book are factual with the exception of the above reference to my literary agent. There is no literary agent in my life as I'm sure you'll come to discover yourself by the time you get somewhere around page twenty- five, or thereabouts.

Welcome to Cuba

"No man has ever seen a land as beautiful as this"

- Christopher Columbus on arriving in Cuba

Cuba had been a place I'd longed to go for many years. The combination of those syncopated rhythms, the food, the fine Cuban people I'd got to know over the years, the colonial architecture and probably most of all the mystique of this strange and tiny thorn in Uncle Sam's side for nearly half a century (and the grudging admiration that it has managed to continually pull it off for all this time) were all factors that drew me to my potential Latin Utopia.

But let's start by saying that Cuba is more than a just the biggest island in the Caribbean. It's a proper full sized, no nonsense country. The length of Britain and bigger than Ireland, it's the seventeenth largest island in the World and a country of paradoxes. While Cuba is firmly rooted in the

Third World its population have an average life expectancy beyond most in the First and a good twenty years advantage over its neighbour Haiti, courtesy a national health service that rivals the very best. It plays host to a US military base at Guantanamo Bay while remaining their sworn and deadly enemy. During the nineteenth and twentieth centuries Cuba was pivotal in World history and the focus of wars fought by World powers such as Spain, England and the United States. And there was that cold one too, the Cuban Missile Crisis which put the planet in the brink of nuclear war as the American and Soviet superpowers tussled for supremacy with Cuba playing the rope in an atomic tug of war.

Cuba's given us many icons. Whether in the shape of Fidel Castro, the World's longest serving political leader who has allegedly survived six hundred assignation attempts, including the infamous CIA exploding cigar plot or Che Guevara who in just one image is recognisable the World over (the iconic photograph by Alberto Korda was taken impromptu at a funeral incidentally and remained private for seven years. This was no staged sitting and justifiably has been described as the most famous photograph ever taken). Try and think of how many political figures have the air of 'cool' that Che still has. We were not here to dwell on the politics though. We were here for some warm weather, a bit of beach and if there's a sprinkle of adventure thrown in, so be it.

Willingly independent, we had nothing but the first few nights hotel reservations arranged. The rest would be three weeks of playing it by ear, making it up as go and as it turned out, wishing for the most part that we'd pre-booked our accommodation the way that all normal people do.

As soon as we stepped out of Jose Marti Airport a particularly attractive young lady beckoned from the crowd of greeters outside, "Hey sexy! You come stay with me!" Aah, these warm hearted Latin welcomes I could get used to. It was December 30th 1994.

Havana

Alison and I checked in to the Hotel Inglaterra in Old Havana after being convinced by our heavily perspiring taxi driver that a tour by chauffeured Lada was the only way to see the island's capital and that he would gladly pick us up at ten the next morning to be our personal guide. I agreed. Well, you would. Who can resist the allure of a sweaty few hours more in a corroding underpowered Russian death trap after a ten hour flight. Lada's are everywhere. Outmoded cast-offs that Fiat no longer wanted to produce, puttering along their way, a long, long way from 'home'. These dreary Russian workhorse's are the standard mode of private transport incongruous under these tropical skies. Old ones, older ones and even stretched limo versions that we presume must be for the 'special people' of the party. The lines of '50s American cars, frozen in time that populate postcards and holiday show montage's is a fantasy though. These seem to be reserved for photo op locations only. As if to make up for it though the Hotel Inglaterra is pure old world charm from a time when the word *'service'* meant something you did as your duty for King and Country and not something you expect to follow the word *customer*. Unfortunately though customer service was a concept yet to reach the staff of the Hotel Inglaterra. Service with a sneer was the best we were likely to get but this was better than no service at all and that is exactly what we got most times. The beautiful and luxurious decor of the hotel seemed paradoxically at odds with *'What do you mean you want breakfast?'* attitude of the Havana hotel we had found in the 1990's. So, eager to get out there and see Havana we hastily unpacked and went for the first time to look at the town that I'd been busting to see for too long.

Walking around Old Havana that afternoon gave us a real feel for the country's history. An English fort guards the way in to Havana from the sea, a legacy of British occupation in 1762. After capturing Cuba from the Spanish we did a straight swap back with them for Florida just a year later. It's almost like those stiff upper lip empire builders sensed that this place might not be worth all the trouble and quite fancied a shot at Miami Beach and Disney World instead. Shots of another sort were clear in the bullet holes that riddle the walls of Fulgencio Batista's old palace, now Fidel's Museum of the Revolution. Spanish colonial style buildings, crumbling and unloved (and collapsing at a rate of one a month often killing occupants within), mix it with Soviet style grey concrete box affairs and stand sombrely defiant of the grandeur of western government owned properties such as the exquisite Spanish embassy. Havana is without doubt on the edge of being one of the world's most beautiful cities. But she's teetering precariously and it looks like no one has paid attention to her looks or needs for a hundred years or more. It's only thirty something years but it really does look like a hundred. On our virgin and hasty DIY tour we were surprised how many new friends we were making. All of them interested in where we came from and offering us the fabulous opportunity to change our US dollars into worthless local currency. And cigars. I'd never thought of myself as looking much like a cigar smoker, but for some reason everyone had me down as a complete addict. Out of curiosity though I went along with the sales pitch from one these Montecristo touts. He told us that his brother works in the factory and if we wanted we could come and see exactly how good the merchandise was. With a strange mix of bravado, stupidity and trepidation we followed him to a building that in its heyday would probably have housed an international sugar trading concern and if it were in London today would almost certainly house the grand embassy of a country wishing to show the world its significance. We're talking *muy impressivo*. Stepping out of the bright Caribbean sunshine and venturing inside it took a moment for our eyes to adjust to the darkness. Above us hung a huge chandelier that probably hadn't seen light in three decades. The walls were dark green, made so by the water trickling gently down and the smell of damp, not cold damp, but a warm smell I was unfamiliar with was extreme. The tout led us up the wide marble staircase. It seemed like a post apocalyptic scene, surreal. This palace was occupied and each room was a complete home to a large extended family of poverty dwellers unaware of their grandiose surroundings, because it's just not so grand any more. And what use are a huge marble fireplace and an immense cut glass chandelier now coated in grime when there are more important things to focus on like feeding a family. Reaching the first floor we came to a room. Our host knocked on the door and after a little chat with the occupant he came back out with a box of exactly what he said he had. Or at least it looked like it to me. Trouble is I know more about the delicate intricacies of tonal differentiation in the dialects of the indigenous people of Mount Denali than I do of overlarge brown fags that look and smell to me like straightened dog's turds. And these were most likely knockoffs anyway. So graciously I thanked him, bade him farewell and we continued our self made tour with me feeling more than a little guilty for his sake that I am not a smoker but had still gone along with his pitch and completely wasted his time. Well, it's my holiday.

Back on the Malecón, the strip that separates Havana and the sea, two boys in particular, one black, one mulatto latched on to us offering to exchange money – everyone wants to swap their Cuban pesos for US dollars and in the end it gets frustrating to constantly say 'no'. We found them generally interesting and interested. At first they thought we were Italian and only after using my finest broken Spanglish it became clear to them that we could be nothing else but

Brits. We talked about music and London and Havana and food and crime. They pointed out, right over there, the spot on the main drag where two German tourists had been robbed and murdered, stripped of everything even their clothes just a few weeks before, leaving the police to deal with the little evidence left with the naked gringo corpses. This I found astonishing, that someone could be so hard up they'd steal the clothes from a dead body. I kept asking for details but for some reason Bob Marley seemed to be the most interesting topic of conversation for the boys. As evening was drawing in, and we didn't particularly feel like a late one on the town, we asked them to take us to a Cuban speciality restaurant of the type I'd seen Adam Faith recommending on TV. These *restaurants* are people's own homes and are able to operate under licence from the Great Bearded One, that citizens may run restaurants from their own homes as long as gringo tourists leave US dollars on the kitchen table. The boys knew exactly what we wanted and took us to one. And there we sat on our first night in Cuba. In a stranger's kitchen, eating off odd mottled crockery, watching a very loud Mexican soap opera on coloured TV. I say *coloured* because it was just one colour. All a mauvey tint of the kind I hadn't seen since watching Emmerdale Farm with my Granddad on his persistently broken TV years before.

"You'll get used to it", he used to say.

"Why?" we'd all think.

This was to be our first taste of real Cuban food. I'd eaten Cuban many times with a Cuban family I stayed with in New York on occasions and that was always delicious. And also in a Cuban restaurant in London which my guidebook recommended to try with the caveat, 'but not before you visit Cuba or you'll come back [from Cuba] disappointed'. Now I'd found out why, the hard way. It was meat and rice, plain and simple. Which meat I couldn't say, but it was from something that had died in vain to make this most appalling refection. To call it Gristle would be unkind to that chewy fatty substance that always brings forth the dilemma, 'Sick it or swallow it? Chuck it or chew?' If only there was a pot plant around like in those old Mellow Birds coffee commercials. Or an indiscriminate pet. No such luck though. The boys however lapped it up. We just chewed what we had and pushed the rest around our plates a bit hoping that nobody would notice. The rice was okay. But how badly can you fuck up rice? Gallantly and after much side of the mouth conferring we put knives and forks together and hoped, dammit prayed, 'Good Lord and Baby Jesus *please* take this filthy muck away'. Nothing happened. The boys' clean plates were whisked away in a flash but ours, mostly still with uneaten dead mammal parts remained. And they hadn't even put their cutlery together. Perhaps a prayer to Satan will do it? And then the out of desperation it struck me.

I stood on my chair, arms aloft and screamed, "Rid my presence of this putrid filth! It is not fit for the devil's dog!" I didn't really say that of course, or stand on my chair. I'm way too polite. Instead with my cutlery I made the sign of a cross on my plate like our native guides had and in a flash my plate was whisked away too. The leftovers would probably be sold to the next poor unfortunate gringos to walk through the door in search of authentic Cuban cuisine, as I'm pretty sure we'd just eaten second-hand food. Or maybe third hand. It was shit.

The two lessons here children are; when you've finished a meal in Cuba don't put your knife and fork together neatly but make a cross with your cutlery, thanking Jesus for your food. And two, you will never *finish* a meal in Cuba. There is not a meal good enough to finish. Instead just ask Jesus or whoever your saviour might be to allow you to survive the night. Gristle is we discovered, the national dish and over the next few weeks we'd better get used to it. Not in the least bit full we paid the bill (for which our two friends received little a commission on naturally) and headed to the hotel for bed, light headed and a few pounds lighter.

At three forty five AM we were woken by furious banging on the door and a man urgently shouting beyond it. I jumped up out of bed, a little disorientated, strange room, strange language, feeling just a little jet lagged I opened the door. A man stood there staring at me, not shouting anymore, just staring silently now but with a look in his eye that screamed 'I am completely deranged - proceed with caution'. He was Cuban, in his mid fifties with wild gravity defying white hair like a Latino Don King. He wore a whitish vest covered in gravy stains and from what I could ascertain at that late hour, patently no access to shaving equipment of any kind. But he said nothing. He just glared at me in my underpants glaring back at him in his stained vest. And still he continued to say nothing.

The standoff continued for what seemed like minutes so hoping to break his saucer eyed stare I asked him, "What?" He didn't reply. He just stood there with his arms by his side, glaring. "What do you want?" I asked again. And again all I got in return was silence. He just continued to stare, trancelike but at me, not through me. Then calmly and for the last time I asked once more, "Tell me. What - do - you - want?" Still he said nothing. He had gone from being Attila the Hun, noisily beating the door down with great purpose to Harpo Marx doing a super silent mime with the volume turned down in a matter of seconds. "Oh dear", I muttered to myself shaking my head. I turned around, closed the door in his starey face and headed back for bed.

"Who was it?" asked Alison.

"Just a man", I replied.

"What did he say?"

"Nothing. Not a word. Go back to sleep". And we did.

We waited the next morning in the lobby for our tour of Havana until eleven o'clock but Ladaboy, the sweaty taxi tour guide who had been so encouraging picking us up from the airport didn't show. I'd generously given him an extra hour to account for LMT (Latin Mean Time) but there was no sign of him. I thought it a rather strange behaviour to close the sale so deftly and then not come round to collect on it until I learned that he probably didn't have any fuel, so consequently couldn't go to work. Oil has become something of a rarity since the collapse of the Eastern Bloc and the USSR's support. This is equally not helped by since the establishment of George Bush's Cuban Democracy Act of 1992. With this the US has effectively discouraged post-Glasnost Russia from sending the black stuff by threatening to cut off aid to them if they do. Less cheque book diplomacy than cheque book piracy. So, with no guided city tour to enjoy we decided to take it on ourselves and look around the shops and see what trinkets, treats and whatnots we could surprise ourselves with. The shops were incredible. Not in the way that the shops in Bond Street are, but because they were bereft of merchandise. They contained absolutely nothing. Fuck all. And yet great lines of people were queuing to get some of it. Beautiful chemist shops with original fittings were stocked - with nada. Boutiques had rail upon rail - of knish. There was even one shop that was so empty we were both clueless as to what it was supposed to sell even if it did have stock. And yet it still had twenty or more assistants ready and waiting over glass cabinets full of air and not much else. Very odd. We bought all we could carry (not a sausage – though a decent banger really would have been a result after last night's meal) and with empty arms went to console our materialistic souls over a cool Mojito (a wicked concoction consisting of about eight gallons of rum, and a little lime, fresh mint and sugar) in a bar called Bodeguita del Medio where Ernest Hemmingway used to muse over why he had such huge headaches the day after drinking here. After a couple of Mojitos each we bumped into the wall, a door and then the two boys from the previous night. They were long in the face. It was New Year's Eve, and they had no beer for tonight's big family party. So, considering I had so much cash still in my pocket after the redundant shopping trip, I gave them twenty dollars. The one whose family was having the party was overjoyed and said we were welcome to join them at their celebration. There would be a salsa band, he played percussion with them. This would be a chance for us, these two adventurous young travellers, that we'd only ever get once in a lifetime. Salsa dancing into the New Year, as guests of a genuinely welcoming Cuban family who want nothing more than the delightful company of some foreigners. We were going to have a real Cuban experience in real Cuba. I said "yes" in an instant before consulting Alison, as I did not wish to break my habit of always thinking I know best. So that was that. New Year's Eve was sorted. We said goodbye to our two friends and walking back to the hotel we found we were still moderately dizzy and becoming completely lost in the darkening, narrowing Havana back streets. Faces peeked from windows and heads peered from doorways. We were conspicuous. We were turning left, left, then right and heading into less and less salubrious surroundings. Then as we turned the last rubbish strewn corner we realised we weren't the only ones lost.

"Paul!"

"Dave?"

"I don't believe it", said an acquaintance of ours of a few years and now close friend Dave Little. Here, lost in Havana 4,652 miles from home we bump into each other in a seedy Havana back street.

Dave is one of London's notoriously eccentric characters that everyone who was 'around at the time' knows. An accomplished and genial graphic artist, he's best known for his groundbreaking record cover artistry on some of the seminal dance music releases of the nineties and more recently for his Votan fashion range. Compact and muscular he could often be seen in the early nineties stopping motionless in the middle of a club dance floor, while full on pumping house anthems were pushing everyone else surrounding him to the limit. Methodically he would reach into his pocket and light a pipe whilst holding an awkward Popeye like pose. Then he would stay there for twenty minutes or so just holding the pose, puffing away while all around him arm waving zombies failed to take notice. Bonkers.

My best recollection of *early* Dave was bumping into him at a weekend do arranged by club runner Nicky Holloway near Euro Disney in France in 1991. Lots of London club faces were there and the next day after Nicky's *big event*, which to be fair was less like a rave than a very noisy wet tent, we went down to the hotel restaurant for lunch.

Nicky's guests, of which we all were, were staying in a sumptuous chateau and as we wandered around looking for our Sunday lunch there was Dave seated in exactly the same position as we'd seen him some fifteen hours before. And in the same clothes too. Further questioning revealed that he was no longer of this world having discovered a patch of magic mushrooms in the chateau grounds at around five that morning. He then amazed everyone by swimming in the outdoor pool immediately afterwards. It was February and very, very cold.

Now in certain circle's pretty well known for his comedy cabaret act, 'Geordie Gunter German Porn Star' in which he struts around a startled audience in a leopard patterned g-string moaning orgasmicly in fake German. "Lickenzeschaft!" he is often heard to cry. And I hear that sometimes they do.

"Are you lost too?" I replied.

"I think so. Mick!" he shouted behind him, "Look who's here". And from further down the street came another three faces familiar from the London nightlife, friends of Dave. "We're going to the Tropicana tonight to see in the New Year, why don't you come?" said Dave. The Tropicana is, if you're unfamiliar, a huge open-air cabaret dinner club and probably the closest you'll get to the wild pre '59 days of mob run casinos and Havana the playground and whorehouse for the Yanks.

"Yeah okay", I said this time slightly looking towards Alison for approval and realising now that we were either double booked or giving ourselves options (depending on whether your glass is half empty or not). We agreed to meet at nine thirty. The house party was starting at seven thirty so it seemed a good idea to try and combine the two. We agreed we'll see them there and returned to the hotel to buy tickets for tonight's Tropicana dinner show complete with charabanc transfer included. The price was $75 each. It sounds expensive for a third world nosh up but compared to what I'd usually pay to be insulted by a London taxi driver after standing in the rain for an hour and a half on New Year's Eve it was a gift. Included in the ticket price was a luxuriant square meal that quite obviously was not going to be like the crap we had had the previous night, champagne and the best kind of entertainment that money can buy. We felt sure our Havana New Year's Eve was going to be a night to remember. And we weren't wrong.

"I'll have two tickets for The Tropicana grand fiesta tonight please", I said to the woman on the front desk of the hotel whose chief and sole purpose on this planet was to peddle tickets such as these. She really had absolutely no other role to fulfil.

"Yessir", she replied, "Is one hundret feefty dollars". This kind of money can buy the whole town here. What must they think of us that we would spend this purely on being entertained for a few hours? If only they knew how much more we'd be spending during the course of the whole evening. Or how much our trip to see their homeland had cost. This must be obscene to them. Whenever I get this thought (which is almost every time I put my hand in my pocket in a third world country to pay over the odds for something we think we're getting cheap), it takes me back to when at seventeen years old I was DJ'ing in a nightclub in Marbella, Spain. I'd watch wealthy Arabs tip a thousand pounds to a waiter after losing £100,000 in the casino next door. Or hear that the running of Saudi Prince Fahd's local palace comes to $200,000 a week and he'd only visited it once in ten years, for a two week stay. At that time I just couldn't grasp it. Only later did I come to understand how it all worked. Einstein was right, it's all relative. And so I gave the woman two one hundred dollar bills and she filled out four thousand forms, in triplicate, twice just to be on the safe side and by the time she was ready to give the two small pieces of paper we required for our big night out it was early February. Well, it seemed like it. But it wasn't long enough to make me forget how much I had given her. So patiently I waited for my $50 change. And waited. And I waited. And then I asked for it.

"You give to me one hundret an' one feefty only", she said.

"No, I gave you two 100 dollar bills, $200."

"No, you give me one hundret an' one feefty only", she repeated.

I argued my point but she remained adamant. So, we argued some more. But she was stubbornly standing her ground. So was I and I knew I was right. Finally realising that this really wasn't going anywhere, without permission and possibly in contravention of hotel guest rules I leaned over the desk, opened her cash drawer and much to her surprise pulled out all the dollars there, and hey, what do you know - only two $100 bills. During this unorthodox procedure by a guest she watched occasionally blinking, and constantly gawping. On presentation of the evidence she conceded the blatant overcharge without any sign of either embarrassment or apology and then had the barefaced cheek to say without the slightest hint of irony, "Enjoy the rest of your evening Meester Mayers". Fucking thieving bitch.

Our first few hours in Havana and so far we've dined out on prime gristle, been woken in the middle of the night by a complete crazed starey eyed lunatic and had an attempted but foiled rip off by the staff of our own hotel. The one place I thought we had sanctuary from the outside world. 'Surely this holiday is just off to a bad start' I thought. It couldn't get worse, could it? No really, could it?

The two boys whose party we were attending collected us at seven in a neighbours beaten up Lada, which was badly driven by an uncle of one of them. We all squished in and headed for the party.

As we crossed under the river away from the centre of town I pointed out to Alison a housing estate of decrepit soviet style high rise blocks, worn by weather and poor design and joked, "I hope it's not in there. It reminds of the Gascoigne Estate in Barking and I wouldn't want to spend New Year *there*, let alone here". You guessed it. We turned left and drove in. The party was in Havana's very own Gascoigne Estate. Instead of broken fifteen-year-old Fords making the place look untidy as in the Barking version, it was scattered with extremely broken but miraculously still running twenty-year-old Ladas. And there was a much lower glass:window ratio in the residences here. Glazed windows appeared to be an unnecessary luxury for most.

The boys lead us up to the family home. Three simple rooms lit by the sort of fluorescent tube that can be seen from the moon.

"Wow!" said Neil Armstrong, "You see that fluorescent tube in that housing estate in Havana?"

"Sure do", replied Buzz, "That place kinda reminds me of the Gascoigne Estate in Barking, you know, in east London. Wouldn't wanna be there tonight."

"You're right again Buzz. You're always right. I'll tell you something though, I'd much rather be freezing my ass off up here in space than being on the Gascoigne Estate right now too".

"Damn right. But wait a minute, if I always get it right, how come I didn't choose the seat closest to the door Neil?"

"You still haven't figured it out yet have you Buzz? Life can be a complete headfuck sometimes".

The fluorescence inside the apartment clearly illuminated the women of the family who were all busily chopping, sawing and preparing finest fried gristle for their guests and the father of the house who was already visibly drunk and clutching a cloudy bottle of home made rum flavoured hooch. It was possible that he was made of Velcro as it seemed impossible to loosen his hug when he greeted me. After several minutes I began to lose the feeling in my arms and was feeling a little light headed myself. I wasn't sure if this was a genuine welcome or he was just using me for support.

"I think he likes you", commented Alison as I loosened his hold using the numerous different coloured neighbours freely wandered in and out behind us as an improvised distraction.

'Maybe it's the band', I thought. Though where they'd set up in this tiny flat I couldn't figure. Soon though all became apparent. There was no band. Just a scratchy old Bob Marley record. I love Bob Marley but this is not what we'd been expecting. This was not turning out to be the salsa flavoured Bacardi ad Cuba we'd been sold over and over in the media. I had taken some time on the way there to explain to the boys that we were going to The Tropicana at nine to meet our English friends and that we'd come back to join their party again afterwards. They seemed agreeable to my plan. Steadily time crept towards the nine o'clock mark and we were still without even a welcome drink in our hands. Much to my chagrin considering the $20 he'd ponced from me earlier. Okay, it's true I offered it but what's wrong with offering your guests some of that drink they'd paid for?

Even a glass of something soft? As time dryly rolled on I announced that we'd soon be leaving. Earlier in the evening when I'd told them we'd be going before nine they said that the bad driving uncle with the borrowed Lada would run us back to the hotel in time to meet the Tropicana bus. Now it seemed to be turning into a different story. They insisted that we stay and eat with them. Nice sentiment I know and an offer that was genuinely appreciated but we had only just eaten deep fried gristle the night before. And of course we'd booked a table with a real meal and the prospect of more succulent home made gristle only heightened the need to be far, far, far away. I asked them if the uncle would be coming soon to take us back. 'Yeah', they nodded and laughed conspiratorially. I asked again a few minutes later but they didn't seem interested in helping. They suggested that it was better for us to stay and listen to some more Bob. I tried again explaining that we had a bus waiting for us and that maybe we should just get a taxi (yeah right), or risk walking back. The 'us trying to leave, them trying to stop us' routine started to get ugly. I protested with the boy whose house it was outside on the landing, away from the party and the other party guests. It was getting heated. Me in bad Spanish, him in better English. The other boy hovered behind me, looming. I kept one eye on him all the time. I wasn't feeling easy about this. Then finally losing patience and seeing I was making no progress I turned to Alison and said, "Right that's it. We're going".

"Are they giving us a lift then?" she asked not entirely understanding the Spanglish row that had been ensuing.

"No, we're walking". Even as I said it I realised what a completely stupid notion this was. We're done up to our New Year nines, very foreign and wealthy looking, escaping a hostile situation and here I am, I'm advocating walking across this dimly lit Beiruti wasteland with the uncertain hope that we'll may make it back alive. Or even clothed.

The boy who's house it was then grabbed me physically and said, "You have to give me twenty dollars, then you can go." I shook him off.

"What? Are you kidding?"

"You must give me twenty dollars. For the party."

"Fuck off". He grabbed me again, and I threatened him. He's overstepped the mark now. It was about to happen anytime now. It's that feeling you get when the adrenaline starts to flow, just before it kicks in and someone gets the snot knocked out of them. To be honest I didn't feel I was in pole position. Heavily outnumbered and frankly probably not nearly as used to this hard level of survival as they were, the reality of the situation was very, very real to me. We were being held hostage for twenty dollars. And without paying it they had no intention of letting us leave. I'd always considered that I might be worth more than that! But because of a mixture of circumstance and stubbornness I was not going to pay up and be the victim of a shakedown. I just wasn't going to be mugged like this. Not on only the second night of our holiday anyway.

One of the neighbours, a small flat nosed white man with the look of a boxer who'd come second once too often stepped swayingly out of his front door. Noticeably drunk and just a little stoned looking too. He staggered over and stepped in between us and said a few words too fast and too slurred for me to understand to our captor. Then he gave me a sleepy eyed look and nodded. "Vamos", he said, *'let's go'*,. Was he beckoning me for a punch up on the cobbles? A tag team slamdown? 'Come on, you and me, now?' Or... yes he was. He was rescuing us. The boy whose party it was, he was not at all happy about this and butted in angrily, shouting and waving his arms trying to prevent him from leading us off. The stoner stopped, pointed his finger at the boy, paused and told him to, roughly translated, 'go fuck himself'. "Venga", he said to us summoning us with left hand, *'Come on'*, and we did. We followed him down to his over-square Russian built van. It resembled a model truck I'd once made at school from a Kellogg's box and then sat on when I got it home. Getting in the back of what can only be described as a utilitarian mode of transport I had a feeling that the occupants of my Kellogg's truck might have been better protected than us. Carefully he drove us back to our hotel. It did cross my mind that the van may not be going back to the hotel. Alison shot me a look that men don't have words for. Maybe we were out of the gristle frying pan into the fire. Perhaps we'd been duped into the van in a double bluff, bluff type, triple bluff sting. Nothing was surprising me now. We had just been held hostage for twenty dollars. However, the stoner didn't kill us either with malice or his under the influence driving. He didn't even try to rob us. I offered him some money, I don't recall how much, (it might have been ironically, the $20 I refused to give kidnap boy) just to thank him for his trouble. But he flatly refused. For the first time since we'd been here someone wanted to do something for us and didn't even want paying. He just wanted to help us and did so not without risk to himself. If not necessarily physically, then certainly socially. He wasn't exactly going to be neighbour of the New Year when he returned home. Maybe my faith in Cuba was about to be restored. And it wasn't even nine o'clock yet. There was still another three hours of 1994 left to go.

The Tropicana bus left ten minutes later than scheduled and we'd made it. We were excited just to be onboard. At last we were doing something laid on purely for tourists. Something where we wouldn't have to think too hard about basic survival tactics. All we had to do was turn up and enjoy ourselves. And we'd got over the first hurdle of turning up almost without even a hitch (if don't count the hostage situation with twent they buck ransom demand and unnerving journey to safety).

Soon we arrived to meet our London friends at The Tropicana, an expansive open-air theatre surrounded by lush palm trees. The stage was massive, encapsulated by great swirling staircases and held the promise of a cabaret extravaganza to rival the best that Paris, Berlin or Las Vegas could offer in their glamour respective heydays. And with no roof too. What a bonus. We were not disappointed either and were treated to the sort of performances that I can only imagine must have thrilled infamous Havana devotees Frank Sinatra, Sam Giancana and Santo Trafficante and other respectable American businessmen on their frequent visits to their very own Caribbean Vegas. The star of the stage show resembled an overweight, overcamp latin Barry Manilow (if this is at all possible to increase the camp volume on our Bazza), apparently inflated to the size of a family house (with double garage and extension) and wearing a blond wig of the sort that still today is still hunted for sport in the hills and forests of the south of the island. I'm sure I saw it wink at me once. His face was powdered matt pastel pink with two round cheeks painted on like a china doll. He looked like a complete fairy but sung like an angel and unless he started to think seriously about his diet, would most probably be one soon. Dozens of spectacularly beautiful girls, lizard thin and wearing entire pink and white ostriches on their heads, paraded rhythmically while El Barry knocked out tune after perfect tune. None of them even remotely familiar, but every single one enjoyable all the same. At around ten thirty our dinner arrived and simultaneously the waitresses extinguished all candles on our table. One of the guys we were with pulled out a lighter and relit the candle but our quick as a flash waitress sprang straight back and blew it out immediately. He struck up his lighter again went to light it once but received a scowl from the waitress who was determined we eat in darkness so instead he held it over his plate in an attempt to identify our last meal of 1994. And even then, bathed in BIC light he couldn't. They'd turned the lights down so the diners could not identify the substandard dross that was about to pass for food. "What is it?" someone asked. Various answers came back. Pork, turkey, spam, ham, something from Bernard Matthews - no Fray Bentos. No one could name the greyish dry meat that sat on our plate. Keeping it company sat two dollops of mashed potato the same light grey colour as the meat and delivered by the plop of a miniature ice cream scoop. For me this was a sad reminder of an inadequate secondary school education punctuated at midday by with even less adequate food. Whatever this food was, no one could say for certain. Some waited for the vegetables to arrive. But I didn't. I knew this was it. Take it or leave it. This is as good as it'll ever get. I had eaten gristle with the homeys so I knew how the land lay. Soon midnight came and nothing could stop El Barry whipping up steam like a queer locomotive heading a runaway train of musical merriment as he sang 'Auld Lang Syne' and we all toasted with our Soviet style regulation size (extra small) measure of Comrade Champagne, 'The Taste of the Old Guard'. Ah, were really living now. This party could go on all night - but it didn't because half an hour later it was all over. Lights on, go home, nothing for you to see here, chairs on tables. A few of the stunning lizard skinny showgirls, stars in El Barry's galaxy of Latin Light Entertainment wandered by our table. Some bald, middle-aged German men who were at the end of our table and smoked cigars the size of U-boat torpedoes for the entire evening beckoned them over and whispered into their delicate light brown ears. The girls giggled playfully. Could this be history's first recorded case of Germanic humour? It must either have been the funniest thing they had ever heard or the phrase 'how does one hundred dollars sound for the night?' was used, as they all left together, arm in arm. Who am I'm kidding, everyone knows that it has been scientifically proven that it is medically impossible for German people to be humorous. (Even the word *'wit'* has no equivalent in the German language. The closest thing to it is *'junenkumpelbumsenheisenschlaffenzen'* which means *'not without intelligent but restrained humour'*). The lizard skinny girls were clearly sold to the highest bidder. How disappointing. Barry's

Babes were just Havana Whores. The only difference now it seemed compared to days when Frank, Santo and Sam sat in the audience, is now these girls are fucking for the benefit of Fidel's Revolution. And they're not unusual. The fact is that the only Cubans you are ever likely to see in a Havana hotel are hotel employees and hookers. They sit around hotel lobbies so the Johns don't have to go too far to find one. And so do the hookers. Prostitutes are allowed to surreptitiously continue trading by the Great Bearded One as they bring to Cuba valuable hard currency. American dollars. In fact they're not dissimilar to the 'dollar shops'. These are shops that only accept US dollars and sell all the things that you can't buy in 'normal' shops with local pesos. These had been recently been introduced selling shampoo, biscuits and band aids and all the things that should be but are not available to normal people, but are not. The dollar shops exist exclusively to accept only the devil's currency, putting them well out of reach of the average Cuban worker who will only ever earn pesos. While ordinary Cubans stand in line for hours to buy nothing with their worthless and tatty pesos, hookers, tourists, diplomats or anyone of those illegal currency traders that stop you in street can spend their crisp dollar bills in a dollar shop and eat shampoo and wash their hair in biscuits to their hearts' content. Just how Messers Marx, Engels, Trotsky and Lenin had imagined it I'm sure. And just what Che would have gladly laid down his life for.

'The Bourgeoisie are prostitutes' he may well have said. Well now he'd be only half right.

After being turfed out of The Tropicana at closing time it was still too early to go to sleep and the first few hours of 1995 were spent wandering around Havana Old Town and savouring the Caribbean moonlight on the city's exquisite facades. We strolled the quiet streets and talked excitedly about the possibility of seeing Fidel Castro give his annual New Year's Anniversary address the next afternoon. January 1st is the official anniversary of the revolution, a sacred date and the location as always is kept secret only to be announced minutes before the event as a security precaution. Heading back to the hotel we took a short cut across the lawn and beneath the arches of Fidel's own Museum of The Revolution. A soldier stood guard with his back to us the other side of the well-groomed lawn we cut across, facing outwards to the road. The museum looked well kept and the grass looked good enough to eat, which judging by the standard of the food we'd seen so far here, was probably why there was a soldier guarding it. I made an observation that he hadn't even noticed us and remember quietly poking fun at his alertness and powers of observation as two slightly drunk foreign types gently staggered past and slipped in behind him, short cutting straight across the middle of the lawn of the great symbol of El Fidel's struggle. We walked on sharing a joke and giggling to ourselves and now with the museum around a hundred yards behind us when we heard a voice calling out to us. We turned to see the soldier who we'd walked behind now heading towards us. Not walking but running full pelt. He was waving for us to stop – which of course we did without hesitation as it was a loaded machine gun that he was waving. When he caught up with us he was babbling angrily, pointing in an accusatory way and seemed extremely agitated about something or other. Something he thought we had done. Cli-click was the sound his machine gun made as he did whatever soldiers do to make that cli-click with their guns just before they start killing things.

"What's he saying?" Alison asked. I wasn't sure. He was babbling franticly. Another then soldier arrived. He was slightly more composed and took over, explaining what the problem had been. My pidgin understanding of Spanish now made me realise the perceived problem that was getting them so uptight.

Completely understanding now and not at all liking what was going on I took the ignorance tack and responded with, "I'm sorry, I don't understand. Do you speak English?" The answer was patently 'No'. So he spelt out the problem in the sort of sign language that even a blind person could grasp.

"Tu", he said pointing at me, "Pee pee", and held his hand close to his crotch with the end of his thumb showing through his first two fingers. He then made a 'Psst' noise, "Alli" (there), and pointed towards the museum. I was indeed correct in my earlier assumption but this didn't make it any better. He's saying that I had urinated on the Museum of the Revolution. And on January 1st too. These two machine gun wielding nineteen year olds would probably be decorated for shooting a couple of capitalistas who dared to piss on the Museum, and indeed the memory of The Revolution today. This sacred day of all days, Cuba's anniversary of victory over capitalism.

The soldier clicked his gun again and for the second time in the same evening I felt the adrenalin surge warning me of another fight or flight situation. I think it was definitely flight this time.

Gritting my teeth and displaying the sort of controlled outrage that Noel Coward may have spewed if a butter fingered waiter had dropped fresh Bishop's Finger in his lap at a tea dance, I replied, "How dare you! I'm British". I turned on my heel, grabbed Alison's hand firmly gave her a yank and dragging her away said, "Come on", through clenched teeth, "Keep walking and don't look back." We walked hard and fast. And of course we looked back. But only when we thought we were slightly smaller targets. The two soldiers were still standing in the same spot watching us go with a bewildered look. A little bemused I dare say. But that was how 1995 began for us too. A little bemusingly.

The next morning in the room we discussed the wonderful time we had been having so far. Gristle, crazed middle of the night awakenings, kidnapping, gristle, extortion, hotel skulduggery, gristle / spam / dollops of grey mash and of course being held at gun point by overexcited uniformed teenagers. I suggested – no, that's not true - I begged Alison that she at least consider my suggestion, as unreasonable as it may have seemed right then. This was a truly one of THE great ideas of our time.

"Look", I said, "we've got all our holiday gear, trunks, lotion and creams - the lot. Let's just get on a plane today and go to Thailand. What do you think? Straight to the airport, plane straight to Bangkok". I was now clearly very desperate.

"But it's too far away", she replied reasonably.

"Yeah, yeah, it's the other side of the world, I know. But I'm not even sure that's far enough. Let's go? *Please?*"

"What about somewhere else in the Caribbean?"

"Not far enough away", I replied.

"Miami?"

"Americans. And English for that matter."

"Hmm, good point", she said, "But we're going to Varadero tomorrow. It'll be different there, out of the city. Away from all this. It can't get any worse now, Paul." No, of course it couldn't.

Varadero

Anxious to leave Havana far behind us we hired a Mexican built Nissan, which I considered a better piece of shit than the Lada that was also available. The booking process took more than three hours as the counter clerk filled reams of paperwork, stamping pages and disappearing into a back room every few minutes to bring back more paperwork to stamp. We selected the premium insurance policy which even included cover against the tyres being stolen. A common problem apparently when the 'raft building and escape to Miami season' is in full swing. We were also warned that petrol may be hard to find too and we should fill up at every available opportunity. I asked for a map but none were available so I settled for verbal directions and we were then shown the way to Varadero.

"It's that way", accompanied with a pointed finger was the highly precise direction offered by the Havanautos employee before turning his back and walking away to continue his paperwork. He was right, it was that way and the motorway that started just outside Havana and was very impressive indeed. Three lanes each way, big wide lanes, with an American style grassy central reservation of sufficient girth to warrant the building of a complete transport system just to get across to the other side. Big, grand and wide, yes. Busy? No. Dogs slept peacefully on the warm blacktop of the fast lane, barely cocking an ear as we whizzed past, swerving hard and screaming energetically, "Fuck me! Did you see that dog?" Occasionally parties of four hundred and seven people club together for a thimble of petrol and cram into a (t)rusty air-conditioning free Lada in the hope that they'll make it to their chosen destination before they all evaporate in the sub tropical heat. Many never make it but occasionally you pass them with their faces pressed against condensated windows chugging along at 7 mph. And when not dodging comatose canines and other near stationary Ladas struggling uphill there are further hazards like the insanely enthusiastic roadside vendors carrying eight hundredweight of onions around their necks who pop up unexpectedly from behind trees on the hard shoulder. Miles pass in relative tranquillity then WHOOSH, up pops another onion man, arms stretched wide and a smile to match like the Two Ronnie's Phantom Raspberry Blower of London Town. Why only onion sellers are here on the road and exactly who comes out on the major national route to purchase onions I can't fathom. But they kept popping up perhaps in case we'd fancy chomping into a raw one en route. Then there's the pot holes. There are lots of them and they're huge. So big that Jules Verne could have written novels about the lost worlds that exist within them.

Unfortunately, those novels would later be turned into poor films starring TV's Doug McLure. And TV's Doug McLure could surely never escape out to this capacious highway south with all its inherent dangers. I loved driving the Cuban motorway. These tend to be the boring fast routes where you miss out the fun in other places. But there was barely a dull moment on our route to the good life of Cuba's seaside playground, Varadero.

Along the way we passed huge billposters with paintings of Castro and Che spouting catchy slogans like *"Socialism or Death"*. That's something I do like about this place, at least you're given a choice. And any country that hangs portraits of Che Guevara more liberally than a sixties stoner in student digs must be pretty cool right? And what of Che? Well ignoring the fact that he was really called the decidedly unglamorous Ernest (Ernesto actually but that sounds almost good), the world's most famous Cuban icon was actually Argentinean. All throughout his revolutionary campaigns he suffered severe asthma, which by anyone's admission isn't exactly a handy attribute for steamy jungle combat. Following victory in Cuba Che was offered a plush post in the new regime. But not content with being rewarded this very comfortable and well earned position in Fidel's new government he returned to fight for all that is good and just (and possibly can be made available at a later time at 'dollar only' shops in other far flung lands). When his life finally ended at the hands of a Mexican soldier in Bolivia he was alleged to have told his executioner, "Come on, kill me. I'm only a man". He did of course know at that point that he was definitely going to die, they'd be no reprieve and that his last words would be recorded for history. It must also be pointed out though that at the moment of his capture by the he was alleged to have said, "Don't shoot! Don't shoot! I am Che Guevara and I am worth much more to you alive than dead!" I weren't so cynical I'd believe this was a jolly nice and considerate gesture to a chap's sworn enemy. Sadly though for Guevara, unconvinced of his self-claimed value the Mexicans killed him anyway. And so it was that Cuba gained a martyr from somebody else's struggle and The Museum of The Revolution gained a Ventolin inhaler for permanent display.

Varadero offered the other side of the 'Communism in Practice' coin. Not romantic in any way, shape or form, just almost practical in a fairly useful but easily forgettable way. This is a basic town that happens to have a nice beach. As a world class resort, which apparently it aspires to be, the mayor of St. Tropez need not worry yet. We checked into the best hotel that had space available. Naturally, we'd not booked a room in advance, that would take the fun out of it. The miserable grey concrete exterior was in stark contrast to the synthetic sixties style once you entered. This was swinging Soviet chic at its purest, cheapest and most repugnant. The colour scheme looked like it had been based on one of Timothy Leary's most vomit inducing nightmares. All the very worst in man made fabrics rubbed shoulders with anything orange, brown or green that could cause a spark. Two single beds that appeared to have been salvaged from a decommissioned Bulgarian submarine and covered in the finest bogey green nylon money could buy, offered little in the way of comfort. No, I'm being generous, there was no comfort. The view from the window looked down on a corrugated iron roofed shanty town below and the poor that are forced to live there. So far I had only seen real buildings made of brick, stone or concrete for citizens to dwell in. But these people looked like they were on the waiting list and nowhere near the op of it. Beyond the crinkly tin roofs and out at sea, oil rigs were creating plumes of smoke all the way to the Caribbean horizon as they burned off excess gas. With this view the unintentional retro decor seemed like light relief.

Night time approached and hoping that at last we would get a decent meal we headed straight for a restaurant described in the useless purple guidebook as the *'finest fish restaurant in Varadero'*. Waves gently lapped the cooling sand and just one block from the beach we found our restaurant. It was like a marine oasis in a desert of thinly disguised gristle. We sat down outside and ordered two cooling beers, safe in the knowledge that just yards away was the world's finest fish supermarket. The Caribbean. The same Caribbean had that served me Flying Fish in Barbados, Red Snapper in St John, Swordfish in Puerto Rico and Lobster in St Croix. Ah, lobster. C'mon baby, let the good times roll. The waitress returned to our table with our drinks and readied her pen in anticipation of what would be surely her largest order of the year so far. Being January the 1st it shouldn't have been too hard to achieve.

"Dos langusta por favor", I asked enthusiastically.

"Lo siento", she replied, "No langusta".

"Ah", I said turning to Alison, "they seem to be out of lobster. How about shrimps? Shrimps? Yes?" I offered. Yes. "Dos camarones por favor".

"No, no camarones hoy". We weren't having much luck. Alison and I conferred and agreed that we'd go for the fish of day, which was a pretty safe bet considering the establishment was called 'El Pescado' - The Fish.

"Dos pescado del dia?"

"No fiss sir."

"No fish?" Is this a joke?

"We hab only chicken", she said with a smile but without a hint of irony. We sighed. If it's one thing we didn't want it was chicken in a restaurant famous for fish. I mean, what is the guarantee that it's really chicken at all? So, we settled on Congri. Black beans and rice and not only was it the most delicious meal we'd had since arrival, it became our staple diet for the rest of the trip. The only thing we could really rely on.

The mystery right then was why can you not get good fish on the biggest island in the Caribbean? Especially in a fish restaurant. Would Havana Fried Chicken only serve lamb? The answer is clear enough though given some thought. Give Hermano a boat and a net and he's in Miami in time for breakfast, waiting tables by lunch dealing real estate by dinner and running for US Senate by the end of the week. A fishing fleet however can clearly be seen out there, hard at work, lights blinking on the twilight horizon. But its government run and the entire catch from these boats seems to go directly abroad to feed the struggling economy, not the starving citizens. With socialist Eastern Europe and Soviet big brother not there anymore to support their former Hispanic satellite in convenient missile lobbing distance of Uncle Sam, Cuba is suffering and suffering bad. The so far unsuccessful US embargo has been in force for more than thirty-five years (bit of a slow starter eh boys?), and due to internal stateside political pressure seems unlikely to be lifted. Even the UN (in a report commissioned in 1994) claimed the embargo was 'totally counterproductive'. Most absurd though is that it's also illegal in the eyes of Uncle Sam for any US company to transact business with any foreign company that does business in Cuba. So if you're a French company that supplies bandages for injured children in Cuba, the US company that supplies your office software or bathroom paper towels to your Paris office is guilty in the US of treason by association, for technically 'trading with the enemy'. Yes, for providing hand towels to a company in France. This makes a lot of careful corporations give little ole Cuba a wide berth indeed even if its children are feeling poorly. In fact it is even illegal for US citizens to visit Cuba as a tourist without contravening the US Trading with the Enemy Act. Now whom are they kidding? These poor bastards are having trouble living off the fat of the land let alone being capable of declaring war on the Land of the Fat. And what is the effect of all this? It's the Cuban people, the normal folks that get a real rough deal (and no bandages), while El Fidel gets a damn good reason for justifiably vilifying 'those bullying Americans' to his people. Now, if the US were to look across to Europe they might see that their dream of bringing down the Soviet Bloc was finally achieved by letting in the consumables that the common people so desired, not keeping them out. Russians were still queuing for over two hours outside McDonald's in Moscow two years after it was originally opened. And a Bay of Pigs style attack could never have caused Czechoslovakia's Velvet Revolution, where not a shot was fired. The Czech change to democracy was more likely caused by a rerun of Dynasty than an attack on the ruling one.

As the Anti Apartheid 'Sanctions Starve Blacks' campaigns of the early eighties proved, the only people likely to be adversely effected by the embargo are the poor. And the Cuban populace is staring a severe malnutrition problem in the face while ninety miles away the world's most wasteful country continues a-wasting. Do you think Senor Castro can't lay his hands on a can of Coke and a juicy 12-ounce steak when he fancies one? If the notion of the US government is to genuinely bring democracy to their island neighbour why isn't this policy being actively pursued in a more responsible way? Get some corporate marketing gurus on it. Midnight airdrops of Pepsi and constant twenty-four hour unjammable broadcasts of Baywatch. Or CIA funded fish restaurants where fish is stocked and then eaten by delighted customers just like me. (It's possible that the last remark was purely selfish, but I've said it and can't retract it now).

Alas my plea comes too late and Congri is by far the most suitable dish for all those who come here until the dissident underground fish movement is properly established.

Leaving the restaurant and stuffed to the gills (though not in the oceanic sense we'd have preferred) we decided to do our standard procedure first night reconnaissance. We walked to the very edge of the town, where the buildings started to run out and we were almost ready to turn back, when we noticed a solitary brightly lit restaurant with just one table occupied. The only customers were two young Cuban ladies and a character that looked completely at odds with the stoic surroundings and yet at the same time was clearly at ease here. In his fifties with head of huge bouffant hair and wearing a lilac leopard print zoot suit, he looked like an eccentric old queen who would probably be leaving all his millions to a cattery. Or a seventies English pop star that time is creeping up on. From an era when it was normal for men to wear eye make up and high heeled silver boots on Top of the Pops.

"Look", I joked, "its Cuba's Gary Glitter".

"Oh yeah", said Alison.

"It looks like him doesn't it".

"It is him", she said.

"Of course it's not", I replied, "Here? What on earth would Gary Glitter, The Leader of the Gang, be doing here?" And then as we got a little closer, it was clear.

"Bloody hell, you're right. It's him. The Leader, here in Varadero. Go over and introduce yourself", I suggested with my hand in the small of her back, gently pushing her forward. Now this is not something that the normally shy Alison was in the habit of doing. And rightly so. Why should two people pretend to know each other just because they are both in the public eye. 'Hello, I'm famous and so are you. So how are the kids?' It just doesn't work. But it was different this time, we were on the edge of a strange and distant place and we'd only recently heard from a friend of Alison's who had been making Mr. Glitter up for a TV appearance, that he was a big fan and would really like to meet her. Actually he'd confessed he quite fancied her and wouldn't mind giving her one.

"Go on, introduce yourself", I said trying again.

"No. I can't".

"Go on. He'll be cool. He wants to meet you anyway. What's the worse that can happen?"

"Okay, okay", she said rather submissively and we walked into the restaurant and right up to The Leader's table.

"Hello", Alison said offering a hand of friendship.

"Hello", he replied looking up from his conversation without a flicker of recognition as to why this very pretty girl was introducing herself, although obviously pleased to see that one was. It was clear that he didn't have a clue who she was and she was forced to make the next move and break the silence.

"I'm Betty Boo", she said. The Leader clicked and then sprung to his feet.

"Of course! How are you? Would you like to sit down? What are you doing here?" he oozed animatedly and with genuine charm. Introductions were made all round, a few convivial glasses of wine scoffed (not by Gary though, he's strictly tee total) and we chatted for a couple of hours like old friends.

"You're in the Gang now", he said with a wink as we were about depart and we all arranged to meet the next day.

Walking back to the hotel at the end of our first Varadero evening we agreed on what a nice man he seemed. Very down to earth and straight, even with his theatrically painted on eyebrows etched somewhere north of where his real ones should be. There was something about him that seemed very *right*. He made us immediately comfortable and

I felt incredibly dumb about thinking he could have be anyone else but the legend that is Gary Glitter - The Leader of the Gang. There's only one Gary Glitter. This man is tattooed on the psyche of every child and parent who ever passed through seventies Britain. He is truly an icon. If not single-handedly inventing Glam Rock, certainly personifying it through his outrageous fashions (with Elton John and others doing the following - though I concede that Bowie and Bolan had more than a slight hand in the creation of Glam too). More importantly though, without ever really being taken too seriously as a bona fide musician at the time he helped shape the sound of pop music for a whole generation to come. There would have been no Adam Ant or Billy Idol without The Leader. His melodies were covered by the Human League, Joan Jett and Oasis and his big bad drum driven masterpieces can still be heard at basketball games and boxing matches as an inspiration to machismo the world over. The only negative point perhaps is that Gary inspired second rate rip off's such as Alvin Stardust. There was only ever room for one Leader but many followed. And when Glam Rock was finally wiped out by the spitting frenzy of London's Punk Rock, Gary Glitter tracks were revered by the bondage wearing pogo-ers too. Gary Glitter's music was tough. Rock n' Roll Part 2? Music to win by.

The next day we checked out the beach. It was our first time to really relax since we'd arrived here in Cuba. As we lay there some local kids came to play in the surf and mess around on the sand. The way all kids love to. They were laughing and having a whale of time. And they would have carried on playing if a uniformed policeman hadn't come on to the beach and dragged them off. You see like hotel lobbies here in Cuba, Cubans are not allowed on the beach. It's strictly reserved for rich foreigners and their whores. I'm not sure if it's a misguided policy for the benefit of tourism or a security measure to prevent further escapees but its ludicrous and sad at the same time.

In the evening we met up with Gary and the Gang at an open-air bar on Varadero's main drag. The bar resembled a quaint detached house where we sat in the front garden surrounded by a white picket fence. Within the perimeters of the fence other western tourists just like us sat at tables, relaxing and comfortably sipping beer or rum in the early evening warmth. On the other side of the fence though was something quite different. Up to forty people crammed themselves up against it. Jostling and elbowing for the best position, the premium point of sale. These locals were promoting themselves to be 'invited' to join a tourist in the bar's commodious garden. Cubans, as just like the hotels and on the beach this bar operated a policy where locals are not allowed inside unless under the invitation of a foreigner. I was beginning to wonder whether I'd had a completely different understanding of communism and equality to the rest of the world. I'm in Animal Farm, I thought. Where all are equal but some of us here seem to be more equal than others. Particularly if like us, you're foreign and carrying dem green dollars. Taking a second look around I realised that the other guests weren't as much like us as I'd thought. They were almost exclusively men, mostly single German men and as a few locals began to get permission to seep through, the other guests became couples; mostly German men with young hookers. Having said that, the crowd outside was more mixed. Teenage rent boys and pimps were apparent and mingled in was the odd chancer with a bottle of cloudy home made rum to sell and obviously under the delusion that some rich foreigner might want this strange brew of unknown concoction, that he held aloft offering it for all of to see. The notion of having a genteel twilight cocktail in the garden had become farther and farther remote as on the other side of the fence the throng was steadily growing into a greater more unmanageable mass. It was uncomfortable to be part of and in no way as relaxing an evening as we thought or liked it to have been. You couldn't ignore it though. These people have been reduced to the humiliating spectacle of putting themselves for sale in the most undignified way. It was a true meat market. And extremely depressing. For a while at least.

But we had our own glitter-shaped ray of sunshine. With The Leader showing that life could be nothing but fun, we tried blank out the goings on around us. We talked of where we might travel to next and Gary seemed to be an encyclopaedia of knowledge concerning Cuba. He told us he spends a few months a year here and anything he didn't know his Cuban friends or girlfriend readily advised on. And all this was in between fascinating tales of backstage parties with Bowie in New York and Groucho Marx in LA.

"Read the book", he kept saying, "It's all in my book".

As Varadero didn't seem to fit our pre-formed vision of Cuba any more than Havana did, we decided to take a couple of excursions using Varadero as our base. Tonight though we were going to have a ball without having to leave town - and we did. We skipped around from place to place finally finishing at a discotheque frequented by mostly locals and witnessing the Macarena for the first time performed by a dance floor full of enthusiastic girls in their late teens and early twenties (though they could have been in their late forties for all I know as Cubans have this indefinable ageless quality). Gary commented to me that he thought this Macarena record was going to be a big hit. I politely agreed but couldn't really see it crossing outside of the Latin market. He even mentioned that he was considering recording it himself. How I learnt you should never underestimate the old masters of pop. It turned out to be the biggest selling record of the *next year* world-wide and I have seen girls in their late teens and early twenties do that same dance in disco's in The Philippines, Canada, Israel and exotic Dartford, Kent.

One deliciously pretty girl stood just opposite me at the bar. She almost looks too young to be in here, but I could see she's not. And anyway I was beginning to lose my thread on ages here. She was nineteen I guess. Maybe twenty-five. She was looking directly at me, which was what caught my attention - when you know, when you 'feel' someone is looking at you. I looked back at her. She appeared to be alone. But girls this pretty are rarely alone. No, she's way too beautiful to alone I thought. She was very slim with long shiny auburn hair and small breasts that were clearly untamed by a bra - and she keeps smiling at me. Politely and slightly uncomfortably I smile back. She smiles some more. I reciprocate, but now I'm feeling more and more awkward as I have my own very beautiful girlfriend to my left. You know, I'm only being friendly. It's not my fault she's gorgeous. If she looked like a truck I wouldn't be any less friendly.

Alison grabbed my arm sharply, "Are you alright?" she asked. I felt like I'd been caught cheating and here I was just being congenial. No. I'm blowing it completely out of proportion; I haven't even gone as far as being friendly. I've just curled the corners of my mouth as a natural reaction to another's smile. But this girl is too pretty. I feel I have trouble brewing. I feel guilty like I've been unfaithful. I realise only now that I'd been conditioned to feel this way.

"Yeah fine", I replied and turned to strike up a conversation with Alison again and put my back to the pretty young Cuban girl. In seconds my paranoia was back into perspective, back in its box and the drinks they did flow. Dances were danced and I barely even noticed the pretty young girl now. Still standing there, still looking over though. Only now catching her occasionally in my peripheral vision, knowing that Alison is unaware and still feeling guilty for being looked at.

As always all good nights have to come to an end and we all rolled out of the club at an unnatural hour to Gary's rented car. Thankfully he doesn't drink anymore although experiencing his driving I'm glad that I did. He has a spatial awareness not normally found in humans that makes for a jittery nerve testing passenger experience. He really is a very poor driver.

Gary does a quick head count before we got in the car and says out loud to himself, "We'll get six in". 'Six?' I think. There are only five of us. Then I see her. Shit, I can't believe it. She's getting in the car with us. The pretty young thing. What the fuck is going on? I make a move to sit in the front but Marie one of Gary's local friend's beats me to it. So, it looks like I'm squashed in the back with Alison, Gary's young lady and *her*. Again I say - What the fuck is going on?

Before we even get the car door open Alison turned to me and said, "It looks like your friend is coming with us". She knew. She'd known all the time. That I'd returned a smile for god's sake! I am making far too much of this. But that didn't make the journey back to the hotel any less uncomfortable. I was last in the back of the car and *she* was between Alison and me. Quite literally. Squashed between us.

I'd experienced Alison's volcanic and irrational jealousy before when I bumped in to a girl I'd met previously in Bangkok a few years earlier called A. I'm not protecting her identity - that's her name. (I resisted the temptation to ask her what her friends caked her for short). I'd got to know her through her mother who owned a business outside Bangkok. After we'd both spent a night out with A and her friends, some trouble broke out between A and another girl as we were leaving a club and I thought it would be wise (as A knew all the bouncers) that she accompany Alsison and I to the front door (and avoid any unnecessary mistaken identity caused, bouncer induced beatings). Alison, after enjoying A's company all night, somehow got the wrong idea on the way out (although I'm not sure what that idea was) and flew into a violent rage that ended in a bitter fight between us back at our hotel. I was cut and scratched to pieces as I tried to defend myself (I still have scars). Eventually I got dressed again, left the room as her temper was not quelling, swearing, as you do after tyoe of row that I would never return. At five thirty am, slightly drunk and marked with sticky congealing blood smeared across my lacerated face, I stumbled across the street into a hotel dining room that was being prepared for breakfast. With the exception of staff I was the only person present. A very polite waiter came over to me and pointed out that dining room was not open for another half an hour. But, then with a handful of serviettes he began to mop the blood from my face. He laughed and asked, 'You have lady trouble?' It felt surreal and as he dabbed my cuts he said I could sit and wait until opening if I wished. He turned on the TV for me, ITN News from London of all things, and I sat lost in thought staring at Trevor McDonald reading the news from home, far away. Still quite stunned by the waiter's unconditional concern and kindness I began to see that this could one day be the back breaker in Alison's and my relationship. A complete stranger will wipe the blood from my face and yet the girl who is supposed to be in love with me doesn't even give me the benefit of the doubt. Or for that matter what that doubt is. Three years later here in the back of Gary's car, almost to the day I felt this eruption might reoccur. And I was scared I tells ya, scared.

For a short distance the back to our hotel was excruciatingly long now and made even longer with Gary at the wheel as every second felt like an hour. It just went on and on, with several near misses, the occasional wrong gear crunch and this girl between us. And all the others were completely oblivious. I still didn't understand why she was there and this too made me uncomfortable. On arrival at our hotel I leapt out of the car like a scalded cat, said my goodbyes and stood well back. The girl got out too, and then Alison. I was still unsure what was going to happen next but then was greatly relieved when the girl slipped back onto the back seat of the car again. She was going home to 'party' with The Leader and friends. And she probably was just smiling at me, as I was friend of her friends.

It was never mentioned by Alison as I'd feared it would be and there was no eruption. There were no misguided accusations and I wasn't beaten up or even scratched beyond all recognition. But then again I did nothing wrong. I only returned a smile.

Cayo Coco

It had been the easiest thing to do so far, almost too easy, but in our hands were two tickets for a three-day excursion to Cayo Coco, 340 miles east of Havana on the Atlantic coast. The booking was made in less than twenty minutes. That was about two hours forty minutes quicker than the car hire fiasco we went through in Havana. Plus we had also booked a day trip to Cayo Largo which had been highly recommended by Gary. He said he likes to sail around there and not just because of the superb turquoise waters and white beaches. Out there he said, pointing to his spiky nylon hairpiece, "I can go al fresco".

We flew to Cayo Coco the next day on an antiquated DC-3 propeller plane, part of the national Cubana fleet and landed in Moron. Personally I wouldn't need three days of beach side pampering as an excuse to fly to a place with such a spectacular name as Moron. It would be worth that ear numbing, bone rattling journey just to see the street signs or tell people I secretly dislike 'I've been to a town named after you'. But Cayo Coco was well worth the trip and travelling via Moron was but a frivolous bonus. Secluded in packaged holidayland for the first time this trip (the first time in years actually) we arrived at a resort development run by a Spanish resort group. Everything was laid on and it was all done properly. A *real* hotel room. A gorgeous beach, a selection of restaurants and for the first time the prospect of food. Real food. Edible stuff in a choice, yes a choice of themed restaurants. We casually made our way to the restaurant that was nearest our room and requested a table for two. The maitre d' asked what name did we book under. Reservations? I hadn't expected it in a big resort like this. There's no outsiders booking up. Surely this must be the most popular of the restaurants then (the least popular surely being the overbland bunfight/buffet) and as such required a reservation. I indicated that we hadn't booked but didn't mind waiting for a table. Impossible we were told, reservations only.

"Okay", I said, "Can we book for tomorrow", thinking that he'll not keep us out two nights running. No, he told us. The restaurant was booked up five days in advance. Five days. We were only staying for three. How hungry were these people here that they'd booked so far in advance? Defeated and deflated we decided to go for one of the second choices after all. But they too were booked. Even the buffet hall didn't have a spare table. Somehow during the planning stages of this multimillion dollar resort some bright spark had decided to incorporate way fewer table settings than there were occupants. At dinnertime every night a gastronomic musical chairs was played and some guests would be going native, going without. And tonight it'll be us. What stunning foresight. Feeling defeated, considering room service now as our only option and still in need of our first proper square meal since we'd arrived in Cuba we dragged ourselves back towards our room. We passed the restaurant again where we'd first been refused and I noticed that the maitre d' was no longer holding the fort and seized upon the opportunity to strike.

"Table for two please", I said.

"Which name Sir?" the replacement asked.

Leaning forward I looked down at the list and said the first name with a '2' next to it, "Rodriguez".

"Rod-ri-guez", she said slowly as she ran her finger down the list of names without the merest hint of suspicion. "Ah here we are Sir. You are a little early though".

"Are we?" I replied innocently, "We'll sit down and have a drink then".

"For two hours?" Silence just hung in the air for just long enough for it to be noticeable.

"Er, any chance of sitting us sooner?" I said obviously grasping for a way out.

"Of course Sir. No problem, follow me". And that was how we got our first decent meal in Cuba. Through pure unapologetic deceit. And what a meal it was. Actually it wasn't great. Piss-poor in fact like a second rate Little Chef 'Hungry Bastard Meal', but that night it shone like a hot cow pie oasis in a sea of old, cold gristle. And we were so happy and full. We retired to our new clean, civilized room, with fresh smelling newly laundered bath towels, a loo sanitised for our protection and scoffed the mints left on the pillows as we watched CNN and MTV in our big comfy bed. Luxury. I wondered, but only for about three seconds what had happened to the Rodriguez's when they arrived for dinner.

We spent the next few days at Cayo Coco lounging on the superb white beach, eating real food, reading, swimming, requisitioning other people's restaurant reservations through cunning and lies and observing the strange rituals of the many French Canadians also residing there. The Quebecois must be the easiest of all nationalities to spot I decided. Obese, like worse dressed Americans and speaking their hooky brand of French loudly so that unsuspecting onlookers could never mistake them for their cross-border cousins, they're a distinctive breed. Strange haircuts too. I had a feeling that the International Hairdressers Association must use them for experimentation.

Leaving Cayo Coco on our journey back to Varadero, via Moron again though unfortunately not through Colon which could have been much more fun writing about ("it was hell passing through Colon with so much luggage" or "Colon was dark by the time we arrived from the dirty back route"), I started the opening lines of this chapter on primitive handheld Psion Organiser. That was January 1995. This sentence is being typed in Eilat, Israel, November 1997 (and I finally concluded it in back in London in September 2006). It's not that I'm a slow writer, but reading Michael Crichton's *Travels'* on the beach at Coco that last day, inspired me to record my own travels as one day someone may find it historically interesting. Well, you're still reading aren't you? The trouble is, a lot of things, mostly unforeseen happened in between then and now that prevented me devoting the time to this journal. But you don't want to know that, you want hear about me swimming with dolphins.

Swimming With Dolphins

Back in Varadero again, just beyond the very edge of town we stumbled upon it quite by accident. At first we thought that that may even have been what it was. An accident. There were about ten or twelve people leaning over a small bridge vying to get a better view of something in the water below. Curious I pulled the blue Nissan over to check what the crowd were grockling at. To my delight it wasn't an accident but a man was leaning in to the water from a flimsy wooden jetty stroking what surely must be an example of the one of the most characterful creatures on the planet, a dolphin. No, two of them. Some others down on the dock leant over and stroked them too or had their pictures taken with them. Scrambling down the bank to get my chance also, I was even more delighted to learn that for $5 I could get in and swim with them. $5! What can you buy for $5? Not even a book about me swimming with them! (Sorry). My clothes were off quicker than Ben Johnson off the blocks at a half price steroid sale. Needing no encouragement whatsoever the only vacillation was that these animals were captive. Well actually they were captive, but within a huge lagoon probably in excess of thirty acres across. So I judged that it was okay.

And anyway it would be a nice experience for them to swim with me.

The dolphin master (the bloke who took my fiver) readied me, first by allowing me to stroke the dolphins and then he invited me to get in. Now, eager as I was there was an element of uncertainty about what I was about to do. Make no mistake these are huge, immensely strong creatures. And I'm well out of my natural habitat. Until you're up close and they're swimming around beneath you, you will have idea of how small, powerless and disadvantaged you feel. I waited a few moments as instructed and then suddenly, with a whoosh of white foamy water two of the dolphins appeared in formation from beneath me, from absolutely nowhere. And as instructed I grabbed the dorsal fins. I was grinning like I had a broom handle between my teeth. It was an incredible feeling. Alison noted without hiding her irritation that she'd never seen me so happy. I don't think I ever had been than at that moment. Although fulfilled of a lifetime's ambition is probably a more accurate description. The dolphins dragged me round in a big circle and dumped back to the dolphin master who then instructed me on what to do next. Just a few seconds notice was all I got before I got dragged around again. I was still grinning like the little boy who never got his fair share of brains. For my last ride he told me to turn around, sit back and hold my feet apart in front of me, as if reclining in a comfortable chair. But I didn't seem to be getting it right. Treading water at the same time my left leg habitually hung slightly lower than my right. Again the dolphin master told me to even out but it just wasn't happening. My leg kept dropping, then very gently from beneath the surface I felt a nudging under my left foot. The dolphin was evening me up with his nose, very gently lifting my left foot up. I was being instructed by an animal. As soon as both feet were level I flew backwards at around 25mph in a big arc and back to base. I was flabbergasted. The dolphin had corrected my position in the water with delicate care and accuracy and synched with the other dolphin before giving me the thrill of a lifetime. It's not until you experience an occurrence like this that you can appreciate exactly how intelligent these marine mammals are. I may be alone here but I personally believe that dolphins are more intelligent than human beings. We worry and scrimp and save and struggle through life but I've never seen a dolphin tied to job he doesn't like or strapped up to the hilt with a mortgage he can't afford. How many dolphins have caused world wars, car crashes, stock market crashes, computer crashes or been bothered to threaten the ecological fabric of our planet? All they do is eat raw tuna, swim, play. They look after their sick and elderly and rescue the occasional drowning sailor. And they made my year. Gotta love the dolphins.

****

Kim's Story

It was 1990 when I met Kim in a nightclub were I was DJing. I was breathless. Kim was a beautiful Vietnamese girl with a superb petite figure and I just had to get to know her. I had wangled a job for Richard Warren my old school friend as official club photographer as he owned an expensive camera and well, he's a friend. Now he was chronicler of events at 'Dartford's Premier Nightspot', Zen (which mostly consisted of some old slapper getting her kit off in the VIP Bar jacuzzi). Never being the most forward person in these instances I asked Richard to help me out.

"Ask her to pose for picture with the DJ will you Rich? I've got to meet her." No problem, picture taken, conversation struck and dinner date arranged I was happy as Larry. (Incidentally who is Larry and what has he got to be so smug about? Bastard.)

We went to the Brompton Brasserie in Fulham for dinner and Kim insisted I tell her about myself. I told what I thought she needed to know, tried to sound worldly and interesting, hoping to progress things to our mutual benefit with the only lie being my name and occupation. I find it's always safer in the first few months of any relationship to give a completely false identity - mine is usually Rupert Gomez, paediatric surgeon. Only kidding. To be honest what I told her didn't amount to much really but it was all true. I insisted that she tell me a little about herself but she was coy. Kim seemed very familiar to me but it wasn't until she told me that she had lived in Los Angeles for a time before coming to London and we talked of places that we both might know did it click. Amazingly I had tried to start this conversation with her three years before in California. Kim had turned me down flat on the dance floor of a nightclub called Wall Street in LA, six thousand miles from where we were now, three years earlier, with a cut to my ego that still makes me cringe now. (I had asked her if she would like to dance with me and she replied that she was 'already dancing, thanks'. Then turned her back). She had no recollection of it but I remembered clearly now, how I got that same feeling when I saw her in LA as I did in Dartford. Small world eh? Or is it all just destiny?

Asking her how she ended up in LA from Vietnam she told me that it wasn't a direct route. The little oriental sex bomb sitting next to me had actually been a nun for a few years (well, imagine that?) and spent nearly two years living in or around Singapore airport before finally getting the money together to come to the US. 'Wow', I thought. So how did you get to Singapore? This she was even more reluctant to tell, but I pushed her on it. There is nothing more exciting than hearing first hand stories from afar. Hesitantly at first, she began to tell me and as her story unfolded, my own life, I became to realise was so far one very long sunny Sunday afternoon in the park.

She had tried to escape from Vietnam on three occasions being successful only on the third. The previous unsuccessful attempts resulted in prison sentences of three months and then six months. If her third attempt had failed she would have received a twelve month sentence as it was standard practice to double the sentence on each repeated capture. Leaving her family behind at sixteen years of age her father forced her to board a fishing boat with two hundred other escapees, including her aunt and her chosen fiancé all in search of a future away from the communist oppression of Vietnam in a new, strange country. Kim was 'Boat People'. After some days afloat in the South China Sea in cramped, unsanitary conditions not entirely suitable for two hundred people, the fishing boat was visited in the dead of night by Thai pirates. Pirating was not an unusual occurrence there during this time, as boats full of escapees usually meant boats full of escapee's life savings and valuables too. The pirates were known for being ruthless but these guys were really motoring tonight. Not content with robbing everyone on board of their meagre possessions, the pirates then systematically raped as many of the women as they could, starting with the younger prettier ones first. I believe Kim may have been victimised this way too though she never said as much and never asked. Some hours into the ordeal Kim helplessly watched as her aunt was raped in front of her. Then when the bastards finished with her casually they slashed her throat, dropped her and let her die. Only six people survived that night from the two hundred that had embarked on a journey only a few days before to what they had hoped was a bright and hopeful new life. Kim was fortunate enough to have been saved by the man her father had chosen to marry her. Understanding that they all would almost certainly die anyway, he tried to convince her, struggled with her and eventually as she persistently resisted his advice he punched her, pushed her and threw her overboard so that at least she might have had some chance of survival. A chance that he and the others certainly would not. Yelling to her over the side in the dark water below he told her grab hold of the rope that ran at water level all the way around the boat and keep her head down, under water and out of sight until it was all over. Kim clung to the rope as he had told her for six hours hiding in the dark sea while the brutality continued above. Her head beneath the surface, only coming up for gasps of air, that would prove just like her brave fiancé had, to be lifesaving. Eventually by dawn believing everybody was now dead the pirates moved on and relieved of possessions Kim was pulled back on the boat by some of the other survivors. They drifted at sea for over a week until they were finally rescued and transported to the sanity and safety of Singapore. During that week what little food the pirates hadn't taken was quickly exhausted and the surviving passengers resorted to the last possible option available in order to survive, having to eat the flesh of their unfortunate fellow passengers who'd been slain.

As she told me this story my whole life experience so far seemed to pale into insignificance. And yet she told it so casually – though admittedly with some reluctance. I was stunned. More than just a little awe-struck as I fumbled for some bread then somewhat insensitively asked the first question that popped into my head.

"What does it taste like?" I blurted out knowing that before it had even left my lips a stupider, more insensitive question could not have possibly been asked.

Kim's reply was without fault and for the first time she changed tempo and snapped back, "What do you think raw meat from a person's leg that has been laying in the sun for a week tastes like?" Hastily I apologised for my lack of tact and Kim smiled and told me it was alright. Leaning back and changing the tone again she lifted her leg up and showed me a faint scar about five inches long on her calf. "I got this that night. Those big fish that aren't fish", she said quaintly.

"Dolphins?" I offered.

"Yes dolphins. There was one that kept trying to push me up when I was holding the rope. Each time I put my head under the water to hide he kept trying to save my life. He thought I was drowning and was trying to save me", she said. The one time when you surely do not need the rare occurrence of a wild animal going out of its way to save a human life was right then. But Kim appreciated the gesture. "It doesn't happen that often you know", she said somewhat nonchalantly. And I wondered whether she was talking about dolphins saving lives or my luck in meeting a person with so much to tell and no visible bitterness displayed when relaying it.

Things with Kim and me didn't work out but I was happy just to know her for that short time and learn her story. Like I said though, gotta love the dolphins.

Trinidad

As we were slightly lost we stopped the car at the tourist information office that sat in a terraced row in quiet non-descript street. I went inside. It was small, dark and bare. Devoid of all the things you usually find in similar establishments in other parts of the world, like leaflets, posters and well, information. All we needed though were directions to the only hotel in town. Behind the counter, surrounded by four strikingly bare walls stood a man who looked like a woman, or a woman that looked like a man. I never did work it out.

"Do you speak English?" I asked.

"No Inglis", was the reply. This being Cuba I was no longer surprised at the complete validity of placing someone who doesn't speak the world's most widely spoken language in a position in the one place in town where they might be needed to use it. So in my best Spanish I asked where the particular hotel that we had reserved our next few nights stay was. We were lost but it was the only hotel in town and I was at the Tourist Information office. Shouldn't be difficult I thought.

"Donde esta Motel Las Cuevas?", I asked. But he/she seemed unable to help. I tried again. *It* shrugged helplessly. I thought back to when we were leaving the Havanautos office asking the way to Varadero and how expert they were at pointing. I thought it would be the same, they had pointy fingers here too, but it just wasn't working. I walked back outside to look at the sign again, just to check that I was in the right place. It said what I thought it did, 'Informacion Turista'. My Spanish was surely good enough to translate that in to English. So feeling it might better to try and find it ourselves I asked for a map. I had got us all the way down here after all, from Havana near the top end, to Trinidad in the south. Finding the only hotel in this pretty little town shouldn't be too hard. I asked for a map but the thing without gender said it had none. None? Not one. Not even one on a bit of string attached that I'd be unable to leave with. 'I'll try the hotel question again', I thought and explained to this government appointed official, an expert in the subject of tourism in the local area that we had a reservation at Las Cuevas, *the* hotel, the only one you have in this town, and that I can't find it using the very poor map that we have. *It* couldn't have been less helpful. Though It did try to be less helpful with great efficiency and just shrugged with barely adequate consolation. 'Aha', I thought, my secret weapon, we have the phone number of the hotel, I'll phone them from here and they can give me the directions. But - wouldn't you know it, there's no phone here. Now forgive me if I'm wrong, but shouldn't the City of Trinidad's tourist information office, an establishment whose prime function is to prise stupid dollar rich foreigners like us from our stupid rich dollars, as well as politely inform us of the delights of the town we might not already know of, just find it a teeny bit useful to have a telephone on the premises? Or perhaps even a single, solitary scrap of paper relating to tourism *or* information? It needn't necessarily be both. Then maybe in some little way they could get on with the job of promoting tourism locally? Shouldn't they as a bare minimum at least know where the only hotel in town is? And maybe have one little map - just one, it could be a small foldout type or one that doesn't necessarily even have to leave the premises – it could be on any one of the bare walls so that weary travellers like us can be shown where we can happily fritter our US dollars on Pina Coladas and Gristle Club Sandwiches? The It thing could scrawl it on the ceiling with its red lipstick for all I care. You know, just for something to do to fill in the months of boredom before the next discombobulated traveller staggers in with a difficult question like, 'where's the hotel?'

If Señor F. Castro were to happen to offer me the position of Minister de Tourism, which I know is not highly likely, I know that Cuba would become the Caribbean's Numero Uno destination within five and a half months flat just by sorting out the simple little things. Like maps in tourist offices and asexual staff that aren't just paid to sit on their arses waiting to turn away tourists confused and empty handed. It would surely be the easiest job in the world given the raw material that is Cuba. But it seemed right then to be just a little too much. Cuba had everything, except maps. And food. And phone lines. And things to buy in shops. And maps. Did I mention maps?

I'd have given £10,000 there and then for one now so I didn't have to return to the car empty handed. The journey to Trinidad from Varadero had not been the most relaxed. Even the last late afternoon stretch, winding through the intoxicatingly picturesque Escambray Mountains, seeing real live cowboys bring a herd of cattle up the road (meaning we had to pull off to the side to let them pass and giving me a chance to get on the roof of the car and take some photographs) and getting a Jamaican station on the car radio only partly eased the tension. The main problems arose when we stopped off at Santa Clara, about half way between Varadero and Trinidad (where with much pomp and ceremony Che Guevara's remains were moved to in 1997). Our original intention was to stop off and get some lunch there. Congri of course. Bring on the beans. It was the only thing we trusted now. We were wise enough by now not to think we could get *real food*, with meat and things. But even Congri was off the menu here. Experience so far had taught us nothing else was worth the risk and so in the first small café we stumbled into, we stayed. With seating overlooking the street we just got comfortable and enjoyed some superb cooling home-made lemonade. It wasn't long however before we became the centre of attention and had a small crowd gathering just to watch us sip. Haven't they ever seen people drink lemonade before? Then I began to feel a little uneasy as within the gathering crowd a few suspect opportunist types began poke out. Time to leave, I thought. This didn't prove as easy as anticipated though. For the first time since we'd arrived, there was now confusion about me wishing to pay in US dollars. Everyone else had been more than happy to accept them but here the waitress had no idea how much our bill was in dollars or even if they were acceptable. She would have to check she told us. We'd been here for nearly two weeks and I hadn't even seen a single note or coin of local currency. And now it appeared that we were in an establishment that had never taken USDs before. Could we really have been the first tourists to set foot in this place? Two tanned, dollar wielding pioneers blazing a trail for a million more shorts wearing, Hawaiian Tropic basted buffoons to follow. We probably were judging by the swelling, inquisitive crowd outside. After much discussion the negotiation was concluded, our dollars were accepted and we hotfooted it back to the parked car which also receiving some attention of its own. I've never seen a bog standard jap box cause so much interest. Clearly this car belonged to the out of towners. Its an oriental rental and its unattended. Hey, back off buddy, those tyres are insured.

Santa Clara has a beautiful colonial Spanish town square with grand municipal buildings and what appeared to be a defunct or at the very least a sadly neglected hotel complete with the scars of war - shrapnel and bullet wounds. This of course was all down to Che and the boys just prior to the expulsion of Sr. Batista. Leaving Santa Clara we must have passed it at least twenty times as we drove round and round looking for an escape route back to the highway. But the guidebook map we had was completely inadequate and the signage was nil. The crowd that earlier gathered at the lemonade café were clearly just as fascinated by the sight of the dark blue Japanese car driving gringos constantly circumnavigating the plaza. Eventually we took a chance and chose one of the many routes out. As luck would have it was the right one and we were on our way again. If all went to plan we would be in Trinidad before nightfall. If it didn't, we expected to make the News at Ten back home within a couple of days in the 'British people believed dead or missing' slot right before the commercial break. This spot is usually reserved for backpackers who think that going for a stroll in the Australian outback without food or drink will be a safe thing to do in the midday sun or beginning a six hour hike up a mountain in shorts and a vest at four in the afternoon will be something to work up an appetite for dinner at seven.

Back in the car the atmosphere between us both was tense which I believe is not an unusual situation when the ingredients of a man, woman and map are combined in a confined metal space. A few terse words were exchanged in the bungled attempt to depart Santa Clara as efficiently as we'd arrived and I believe arms were indeed folded. Not by me obviously. I was driving. But even in the tropical sunshine things had turned icy. It was similar to how it might have been if the surprise star turn at a pre-war bat mitzvah turned out to be a young Adolf Schicklgruber and his amazing Aryan glove puppet, Zeigy. Still, after the winding road through the Escambray Mountains, the passing gaucho's (who resembled more than a passing resemblance to six singularly themed Village People) and the Ragga soundtrack being blasted in from across the sea, we arrived in Trinidad. And it was a sight for sore eyes.

Trinidad's the town they always show on the tourist board advertisements. 'Come to Cuba. Where $20 kidnapping is just part of the fun'. Or in Vogue photo shoots and magazine campaigns for rum that's really produced under licence in a factory in Rotherham. Quaint cobbled streets edged in by even quainter tiled roofed buildings, the walls painted in pastel hues that throb and come alive in the early evening glow climb the hills that look out over the blue Caribbean sea just below. Castro's administration demanded a complete restoration of the town (something that Havana and in turn the Cuban tourist information office's could benefit from too) and since 1988 has been listed as a UNESCO World Heritage Site. And let me tell you now, those UNESCO folks know their stuff. Trinidad is remarkable. At last we thought, we had found the Cuba that so far had eluded us.

Trinidad was founded in 1514 as a set off point for Spanish expeditions into the New World. A great place to recharge the batteries after an Atlantic crossing, before going off to unknown lands to kill people who have lived peacefully and in harmony with the land for generations. Hernando Cortés set out from here to conquer Mexico in 1518 and discovered that the Aztec Emperor Montezuma regarded him as a reincarnation of the god Quetzalcoatl. Cortés must have been most pleasantly surprised when the Aztec's greeted them on the beach with welcoming gifts of gold, food, fine cotton garments, finery and several young women. Well, what sailor wouldn't be pleasantly surprised? The Spanish had arrived in boats that perfectly fitted a description told in a prophecy of Quetzalcoatl's arrival many years before and the Aztec's had been waiting their arrival. Cortés obviously didn't want to disappoint his hosts so he gratefully accepted the gifts and in return gave them a chair and a crimson hat on behalf of the Spanish king Yes a chair and a hat. Cortés asked if he could meet the Aztec emperor to personally present the gifts and the greeting party agreed and lead him to Montezuma to make his chair and hat presentation. Once Cortés and his men were comfortably installed inside the emperor's palace he repaid his host's generosity by holding him ransom and then killing as many Aztecs as he possibly could by launching his attack from within. This was of course standard procedure in these times. Make friends, accept gifts, kill them mercilessly, go home richer. How things have changed in three and a half centuries. No civilised government would travel around the world, topple a leader and steal the country's wealth and resources in this day and age, would they?

Back then Trinidad was a glorious place, a launch pad for adventure marking the start of great conquests into the unknown and the discovery far off lands. How things have changed. Now they're not even able to offer suitable directions to the nearest hotel. Even without the 'androgynous tourist thing from hell's' help we eventually found our accommodation, Motel Las Cuevas. A series of semi-detached annexed bungalows with a bar terrace to enjoy early evening mojito's while the sun sets over the prettiest town in Cuba.

Having earlier spotted a comely little restaurant in town on the way up to the hotel, where the staff were friendly, a small band banged out some salsa and the atmosphere was everything we'd expected from Cuba but so far hadn't experienced, we reserved a table for later that evening and decided to forgo queuing at the 'Lenin Lounge Buffet of the Revolution' at Las Cuevas for a scrap of fried goat skin (it was Tuesday so the gristle was off). As evening drew in we walked down to the restaurant greatly anticipating the night ahead and the band we'd seen playing earlier. Although the moon was full and lit the cobblestones, Trinidad was a dark place. No street lighting could be seen and as we walked past houses we peeked a glance through the open balustraded windows into a different life from a different time. Many of the houses had antique furniture and strangely just like the street outside, no electricity. It was just like the city had been frozen in the early 1820's, but eerily it reminded us as we walked of what it must have been like in Roman times or an era before electricity, gas, microwaves or motor vehicles. There was that kind of weird ancient feel about the place as we walked through the town in total darkness. Every now and then we'd see someone lurking in the shadows or a doorway. Only the glow of a cigarette would give away their position. Finally we turned the corner where the restaurant we'd seen and booked earlier was situated. Dark and shuttered, it was closed. And we were gutted. Well, we thought, 'Buffet of the Revolution' it is then. We idled our way back up the hill to Las Cuevas only to find the 'Revolution' was over, packed up, cleared away. All the freedom fighters had retreated to their beds or the bar leaving not a scrap of crappy food for us. We asked at the hotel reception whether there was a possibility of getting provisions after our long and hungry day of travels. Remember, we couldn't get any lunch in Santa Clara either. The night manager laughed and told us we shouldn't have gone out in the first place and that there was no way we would have got any food in town during a power cut. Power cut! This wasn't a fascinating step back in ancient time. It was a electrical fault. And the serving of food was well over at Las Cuevas. There was nothing to eat at the inn. The cupboards were bare. The chef had died. To be fair I don't remember the exact excuse not to sell us food but we weren't getting any. Couldn't even get a slice of dry bread. We retreated to the bar reassuring ourselves that at least tonight had been the best culinary evening we had so far experienced in Cuba. And tomorrow would be the best cold egg breakfast we'd ever eat for sure. We went to bed, tired and once again very, very hungry.

The next day we explored Trinidad including the exquisitely named Romantic Museum. An odd exhibit in a socialist state, the former home of a Spanish Count, Count Brunet if you really want to know and the museum is filled with furniture and paintings of a strictly bourgeois nature.

Many of the works of art celebrate the joys of slavery and exploitative sugar wealth. In each room guarding these priceless relics of an age gone by, sits a curator. Each a middle aged woman, of every colour, and every last one is busy doing the same thing, crocheting lace table mats.

I asked one, a friendly faced woman in the bestest Spanish I could muster, "Cuál está éste en español?", sort of *What is it in Spanish?'* Curious as to the translation of 'crochet' or 'crocheting' and pointing to her delicate handiwork.

She looked up at me and said matter of factly, but with a smile while holding up her work for me to see, "Doily". And it was indeed a Doily.

Escape to Havana

We'd enjoyed our brief trip to Trinidad more than anywhere else in Cuba. Even if we never had the opportunity to eat. Perhaps we were delirious from starvation but to me it seemed suitably laid back, pleasing on the eye and surprisingly hassle free. We enjoyed just sitting on a bench in the town square watching men lead mules laden with stock. The atmosphere of Trinidad, like the buildings, seemed to be from another era. Poverty was still apparent but life for the Trinidadians seemed easier to contend with than their compatriots in Havana. We were never asked outright for money, but sadly one woman, sobbing and filthy stopped us asking for soap. Not a beggar like you might see in London asking for cash to score drugs. But a human being, someone's mother with her hand out, tears in her eyes reduced to beg for soap. It saddened me to the bottom of my soul that just a few hundred miles away there is a governing administration that can consciously refuse a woman and a her children a simple and common necessity such as soap, hoping that it will bring the collapse of the Castro regime. I have spoken with Cubans in the US and non-Cubans who believe the embargo by the US government should continue and that it will eventually work.

But none of them could have looked in the sad eyes and seen the out stretched hand of a woman who had to degrade herself to beg for a bar of soap.

Sadly leaving Trinidad behind we headed back to Havana on the big empty highway that had introduced us to Varadero, Gary Glitter, Santa Clara and Trinidad. Half an hour into our drive, like a mirage in the motorway's vast central reservation we saw a small hut made of wood with a thatched roof and standing on high stilts. Above it was a huge sign in the shape of a steaming coffee cup and it was beckoning us in. We didn't even have to consult on this one. Breakfast at Las Cuevas was not the feast we'd dreamed about the night before and a good stirring java would certainly get us through journey ahead. Let me clarify that; when I said it wasn't a feast, what I meant was, 'it wasn't anything'. We set out early and the hotel had decided that today would be a good day to open the breakfast hall two and a half hours later than usual and this didn't completely fit in with our schedule. So we checked out once more on empty stomachs. Something that was beginning to feel normal and perhaps something the Cuban people experience more regularly than we ever will. Were we experiencing their normality? The imaginary aroma of coffee from the giant steaming cup drew us closer like in skag addicts on a free field trip to Afghanistan. We pulled in. The rest stop was surprisingly modern and civilised and would not be out of place on the roadside in France or Italy. Except that ours was the only car there. We parked in the shade and walked up the wooden steps to the bar. With a wave of relief I ordered two white coffees. One of the four men in immaculately pressed white uniforms behind the bar (twice the current clientele) smiled at me and told me shaking his head that there was no milk. We laughed. They laughed too. So we laughed back just to get the last laugh in. Two black coffees then? Like a flashback to our first night in Varadero at the fish restaurant he told me, sorry, there was no coffee either. I did a comic double take at the steaming coffee cup sign.

He laughed again and said, "Welcome to Cuba". Perhaps he meant, 'Cuba, you're welcome to it.' We didn't care now. We weren't at home. We hadn't got anything we wanted in three weeks of asking and expectation and so the breakfast we had that day on the roadside, made of Coca Cola and Hot Dogs was possibly the most welcome and nutritious meal I had ever enjoyed. I wanted it to go on forever. It was bliss. Taking a stock of extra Coke's for the journey we made our way back to the highway and onward to Havana filled with the goodness of a pure sugar, caffeine, white bread and minced animal lips fuelling us on. We avoided the sleeping dogs in the fast lane with the self-confidence of experienced and worldly wise travellers. We were on our way. Just a couple of more days in Havana and we'd be heading home to gloomy January London. I don't think I have ever looked forward to something so much since childhood Christmases. It's warm here in Cuba and the palm trees look good but the pressure is constant. It may seem weird wanting to leave the sunny Caribbean shores for an English winter. I'd never felt like that before. But always having to fob off hustlers, beggars, money changers, cigar peddlers and con artists makes you weary. This was hard work.

So for our last few days back in Havana (never having to give up our tyres to a rafter by the way) we avoided the streets outside and spent time at the pool of Hotel Sevilla with Gary and occasionally a member of the British Embassy staff, our man in Havana. I broke the unfortunate news that comic genius Peter Cook had died. Gary mused, sadly gazing distantly into the distance, "I once woke up in the same bed with him". Must have been one hell of a party.

It was nearly over and for our last night we met up with Gary, Dave Little and his friends for a farewell dinner. The evening ended with Gary leading the whole restaurant with an impromptu rendition of Rock 'n' Roll Part 1 into a conga around the tables, emptying every table of patrons out the door into the street and finally back to our tables again. The serenading minstrels who Gary had requisitioned the guitar from, looked on in helpless bemusement. 'Who is this crazy wig wearing gringo with my guitar? Why do they follow him like that? We must learn those numbers!' (Right now there is a band of Havana troubadours obliviously singing 'Do You Wanna Touch' to a highly embarrassed Canadian couple who are trying to enjoy a quiet, romantic dinner but far too polite to shoo them away). The restaurant staff panicked momentarily thinking it was an elaborate ruse to bilk the bill and only relaxed when The Leader led the entire clientele back from the street and into to their seats again. That evening was a great way to kiss Havana 'Adios'. We went to Cuba alone hoping to find the Latin romance, the heat and rhythm of a Celia Cruz song, but left dancing around with a bunch of other English reprobates to a Gary Glitter tune that consisted of mostly grunts. English people. Can't take 'em anywhere.

If I had to describe my feelings toward Cuba I'd honestly say that this island, the biggest in the Caribbean, the same length as Britain in fact, has by far the most untapped potential in the region. Cuba is more than a satellite state of an Old World that no longer cares, but a nation with incredible history, which at times has played a pivotal role in world events and one with incredible resources if only it could fully utilise them. It's a proper country, not an 'island'.

Geologically Cuba has been blessed, mountains, coast and everything in between is rich even if the people that farm the land aren't. Cayo Largo has one the world's great beaches (and as an unexpected bonus definitely the funkiest airport that at night doubles up as a disco after dark. I kid you not. It's the only airport lounge I've ever been in with flashing lights, dance floor, turntables, mixer and a full on sound system.) Columbus wasn't wrong when he said how beautiful this land was. But he came before the US trade embargo. The people of Cuba are resourceful, keeping fleets ancient cars going with no parts supply and they can hustle with the best of them while living on meagre rations and without the promise of any great future ahead of them. Cuba has so much to offer. So much that is unexploited. So much abusively ignored or criminally underexposed. But the feeling we had of no longer wanting to explore the streets of the city because you don't want to constantly rebuff 'money changers', hustlers or potential thieves does not make a relaxed atmosphere or an ideal holiday. The appalling food and lack of supply is not only disappointing for the visitor (safe in the knowledge they can return home), but truly depressing when you see that natives readily accept this as the norm. More so when you know how close physically the world of wasteful abundance is. Is it any wonder that so many Cubans long for life and the never-ending buffet table of the US of A?

More than most things I think I missed the music that wasn't there. I wanted to hear Benny Moré and Celia Cruz. Instead all we got was the big hit of the time from Ace of Base; Swedish pop reggae. I hear more salsa in an average London day than a Cuban fortnight. One of Cuba's great treasures is its musical heritage. An embodiment of the nation which to my mind spearheads the Cuban identity to the outside world, sets it apart from the rest of the Caribbean and Latin America and justifiably staking its a claim to be one the world's great and individual nations. It's the tip of an iceberg that says, 'This is Cuba. It's unmistakable'. Cuba is after all unique.

In time Cuba will be one *the* great places to visit. It almost has it all. But for now regrettably, almost is not enough and as long the current external political situation forces the hand of the internal. It's not one of the great places to visit yet. Waste two weeks of your life elsewhere if you have two weeks to spare. Because for now, Cuba's just Poland with palm trees.

Printed in the United Kingdom
by Lightning Source UK Ltd.
134683UK00002B/223-225/P